Let's dive into the world of Colouring and Doodling!

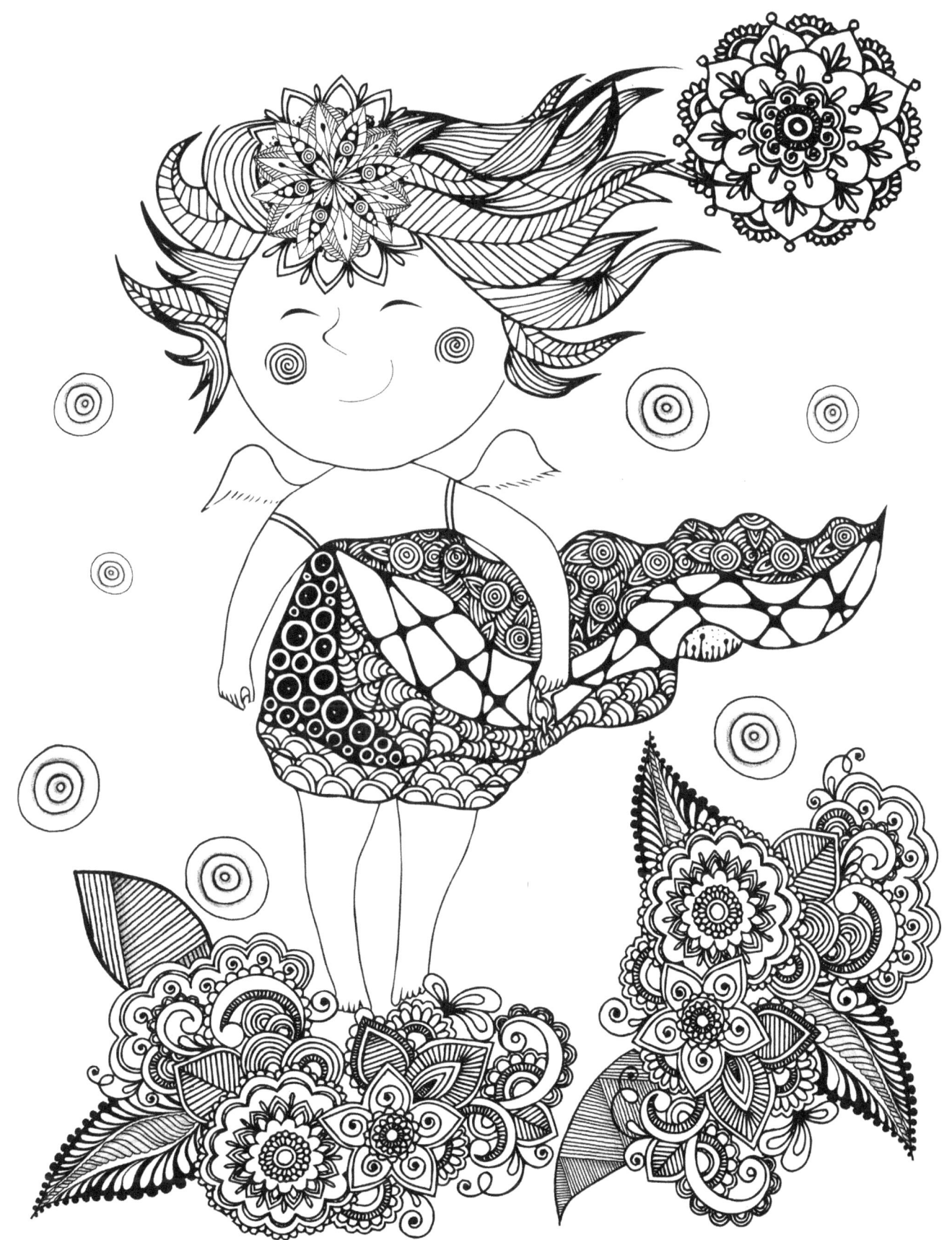

Art is the daughter of freedom.
Friedrich Schiller

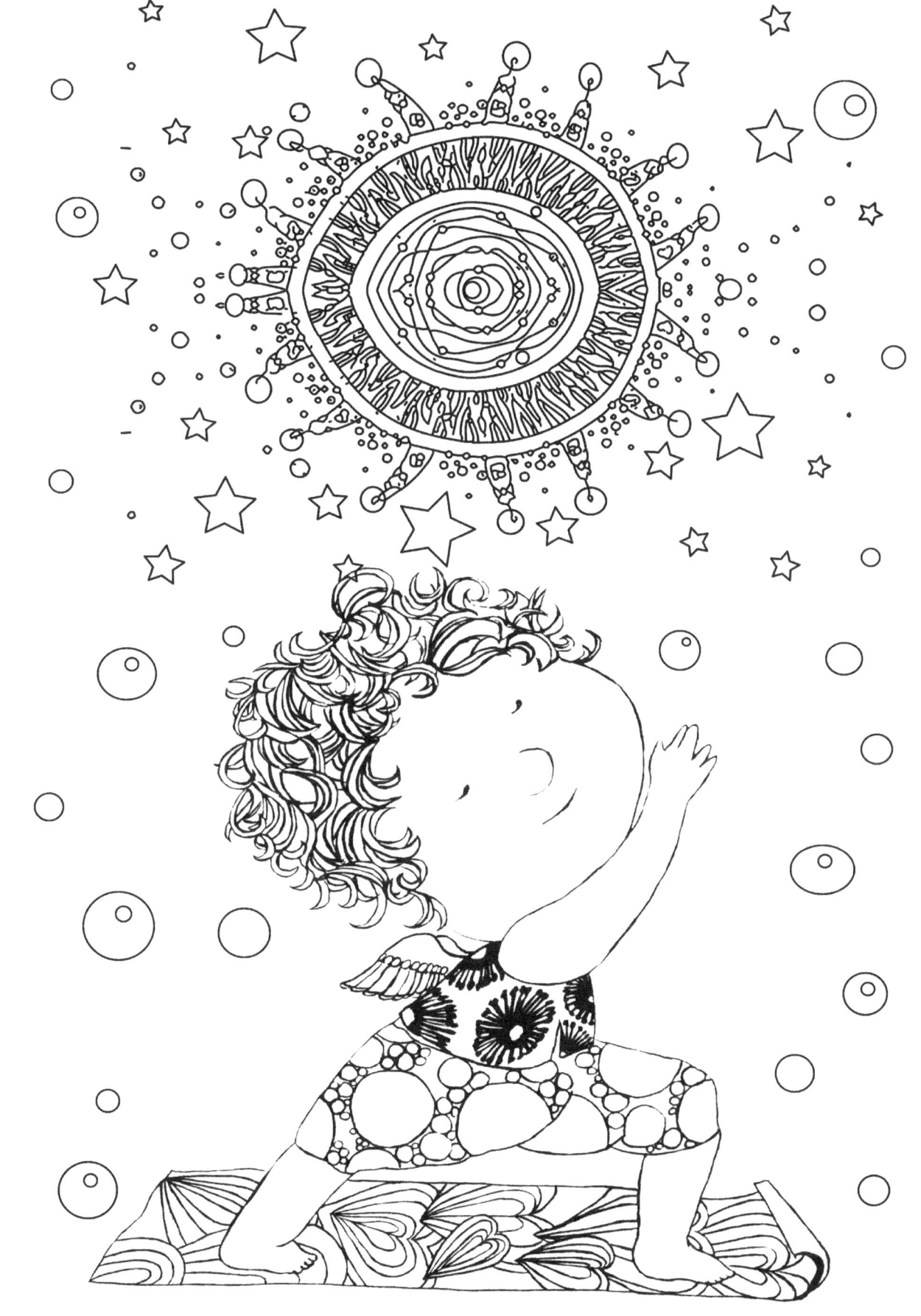

Do not dwell in the past, do not dream of the future,
concentrate the mind on the present moment.
Buddha

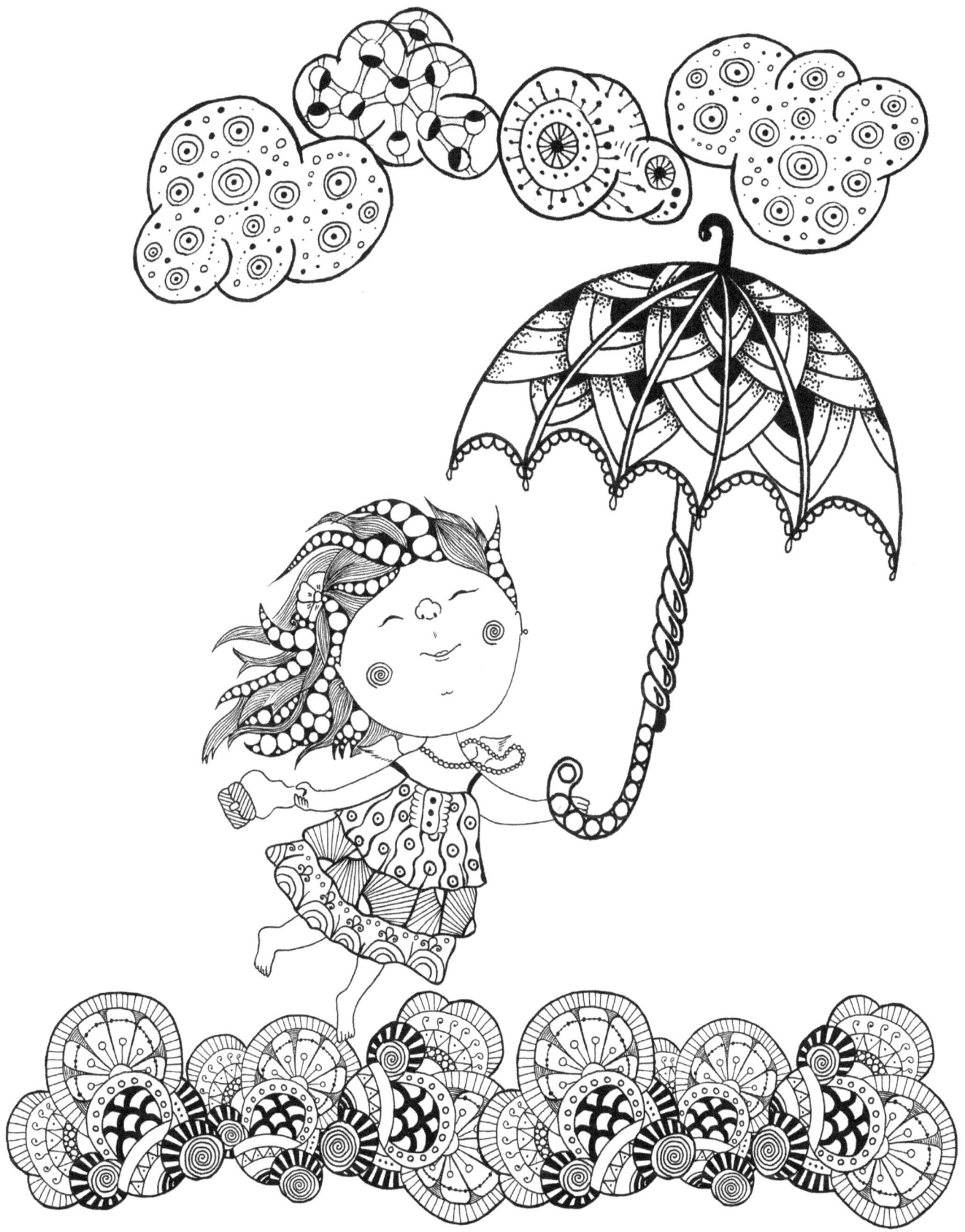

I can't change the direction of the wind,
but I can adjust my sails to always reach my destination.
Jimmy Dean

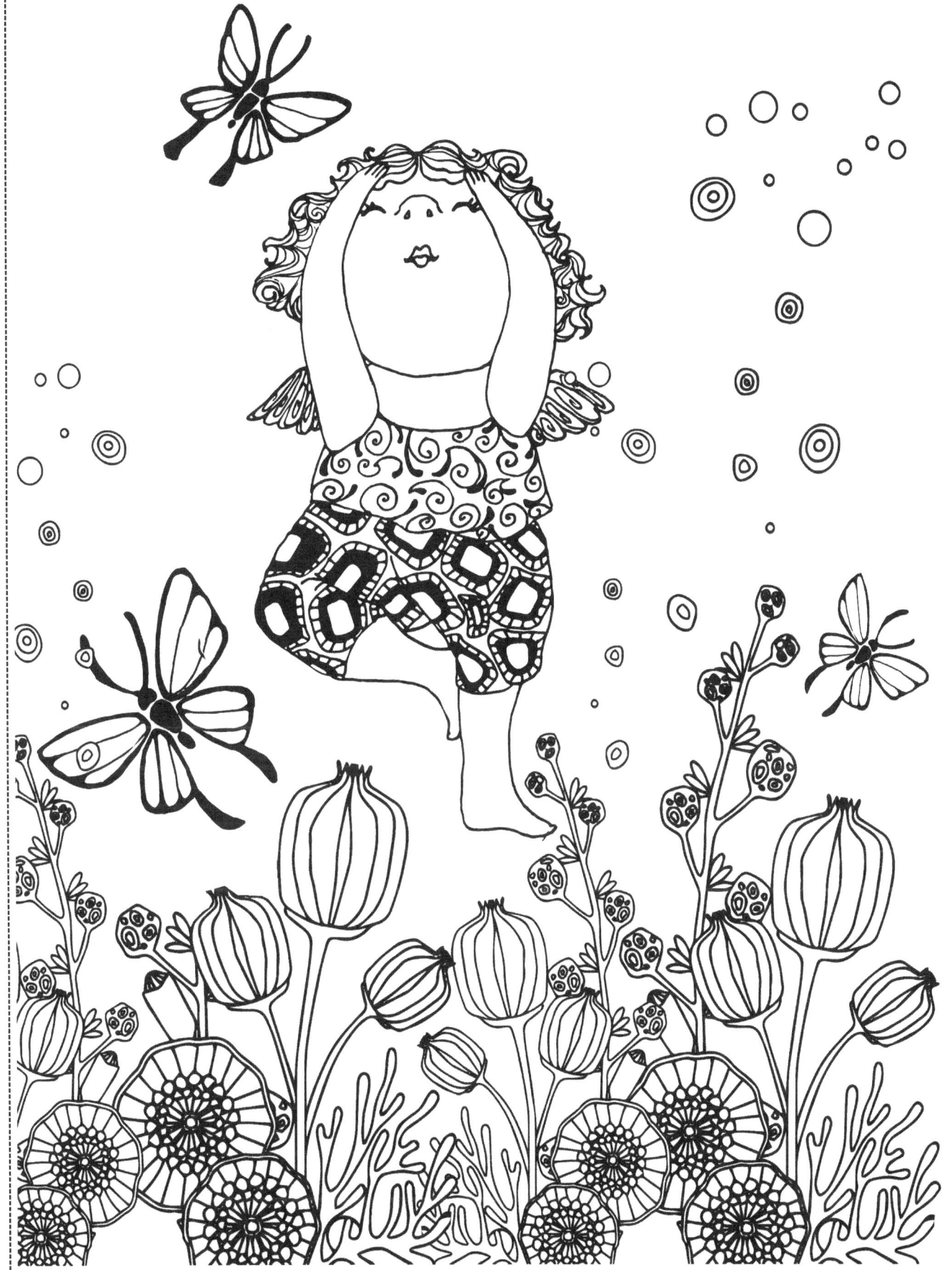

Keep your face always toward the sunshine –
and shadows will fall behind you.
Walt Whitman

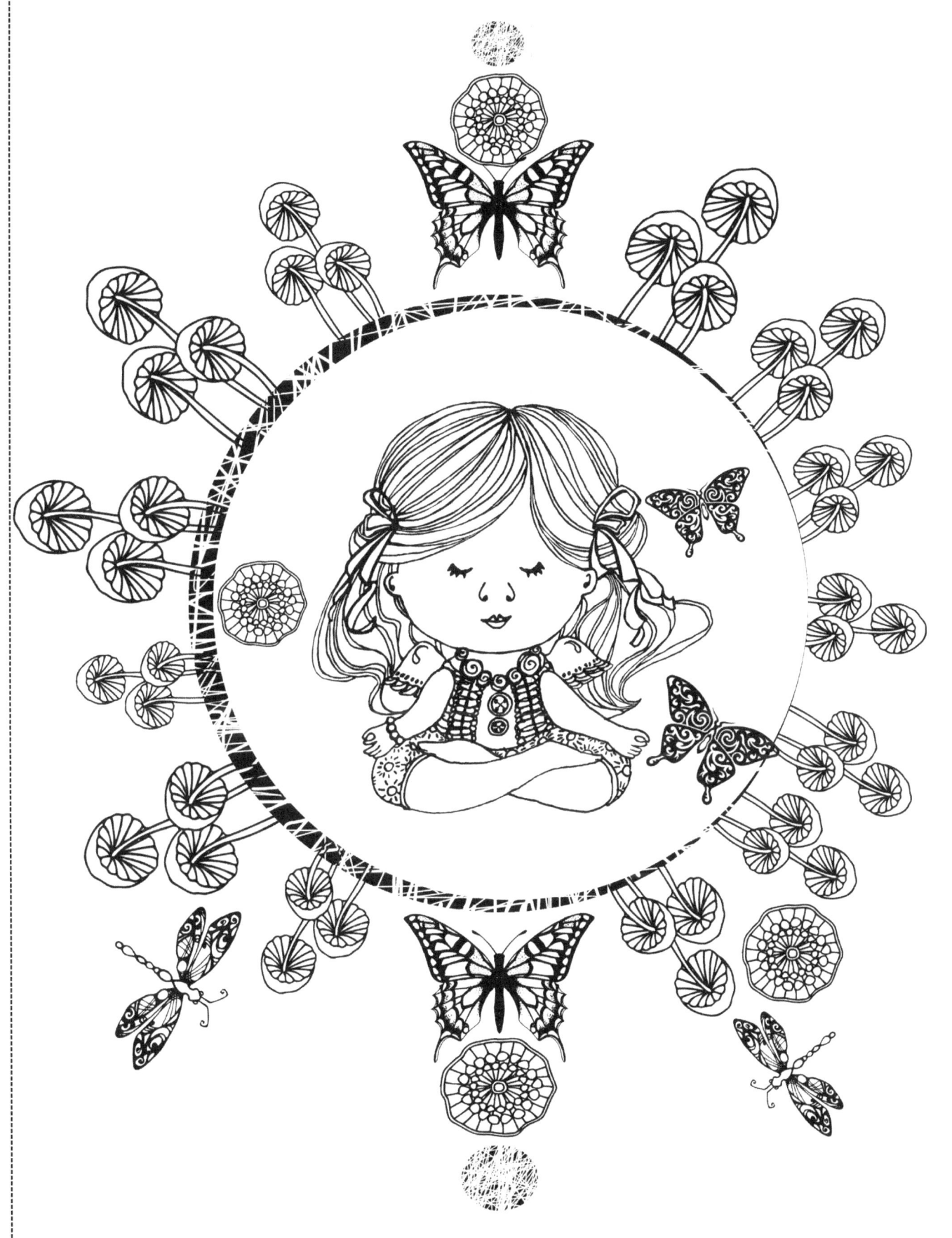

What we think, we become.

Buddha

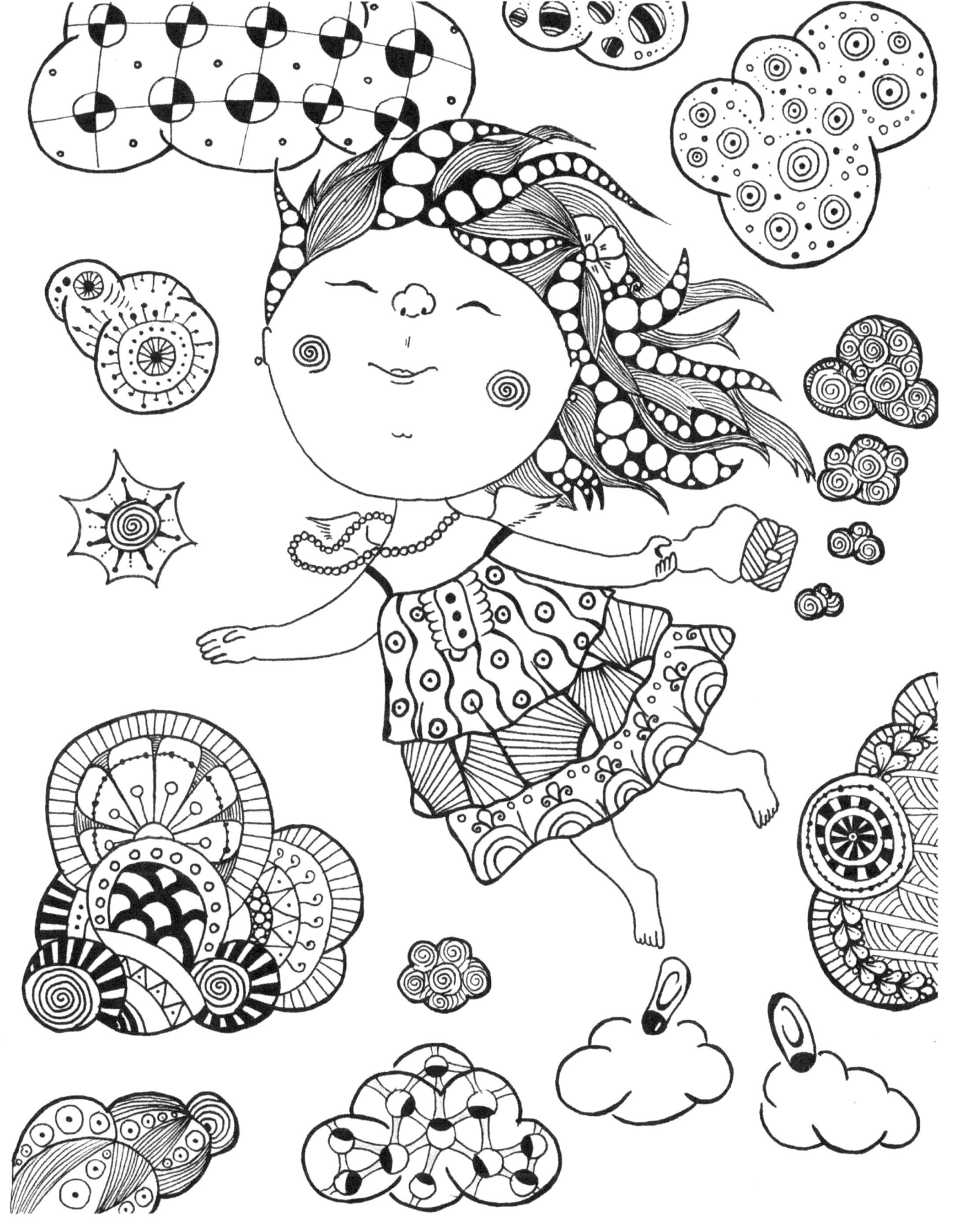

My mission in life is not merely to survive, but to thrive; and to do so with some passion, some compassion, some humor, and some style.
Maya Angelou

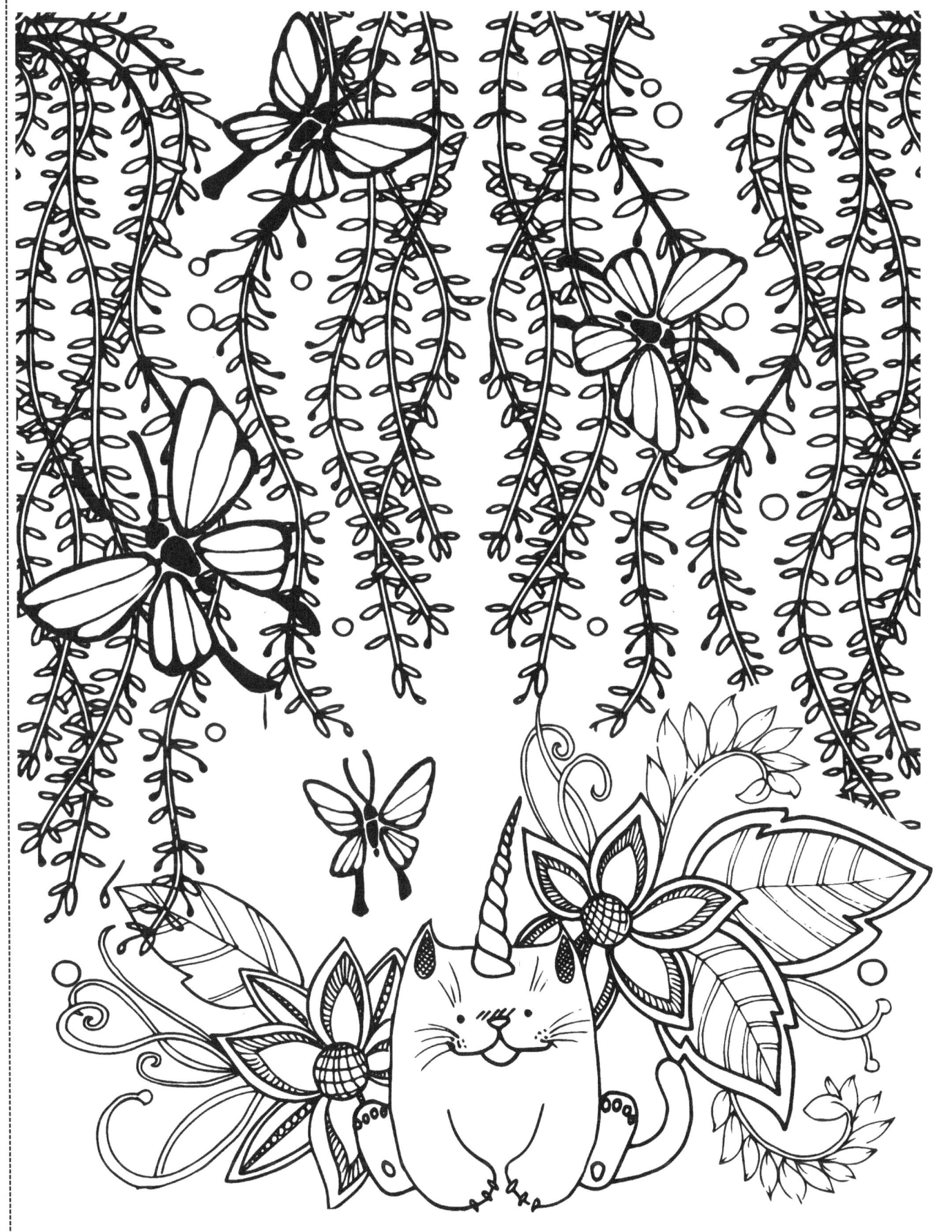

It is very inconvenient habit of kittens that,
whatever you say to them they always purr.
Lewis Carroll

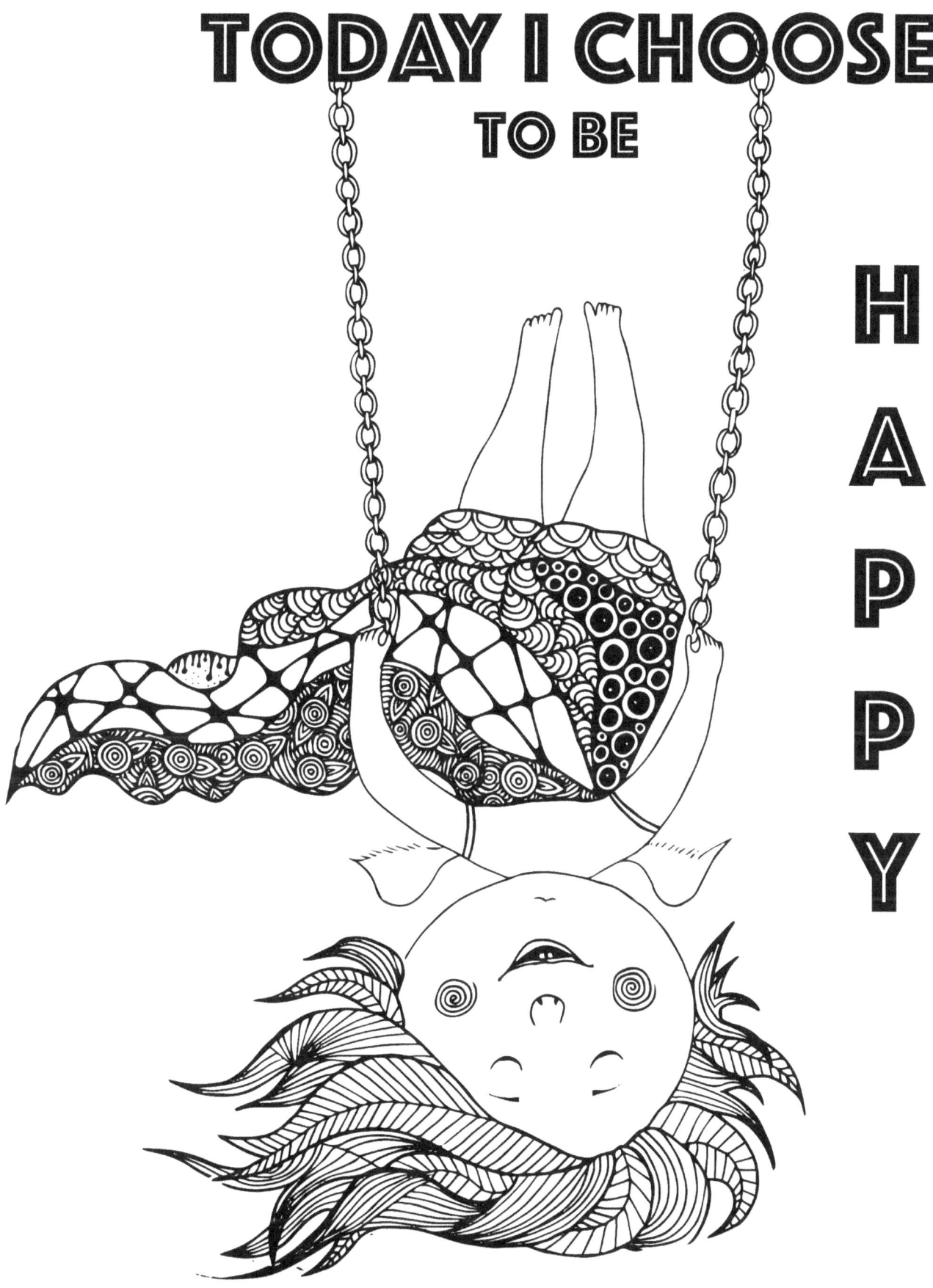

Live life to the fullest, and focus on the positive.
Matt Cameron

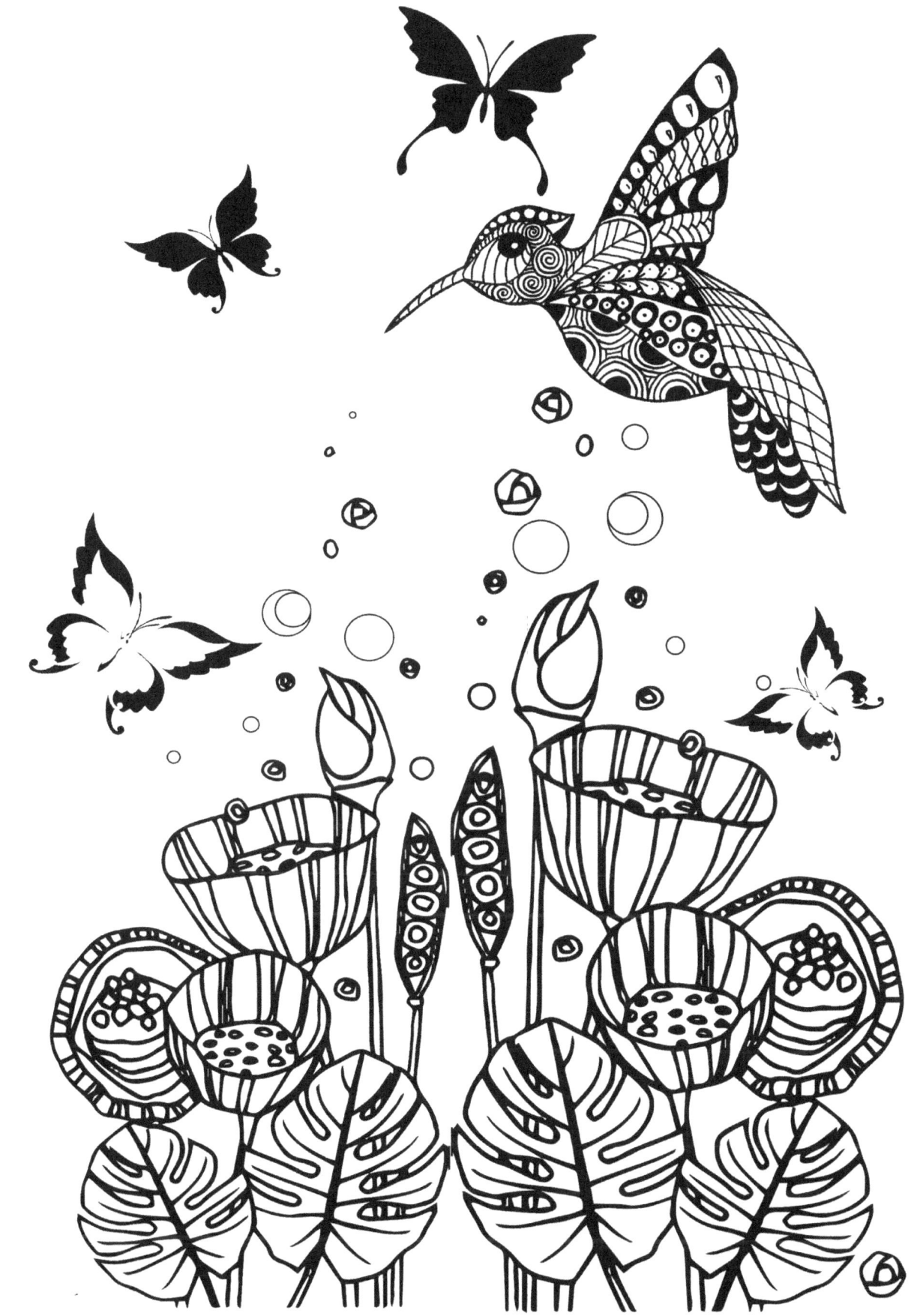

Always remember that you are absolutely unique.
Just like everyone else.
Margaret Mead

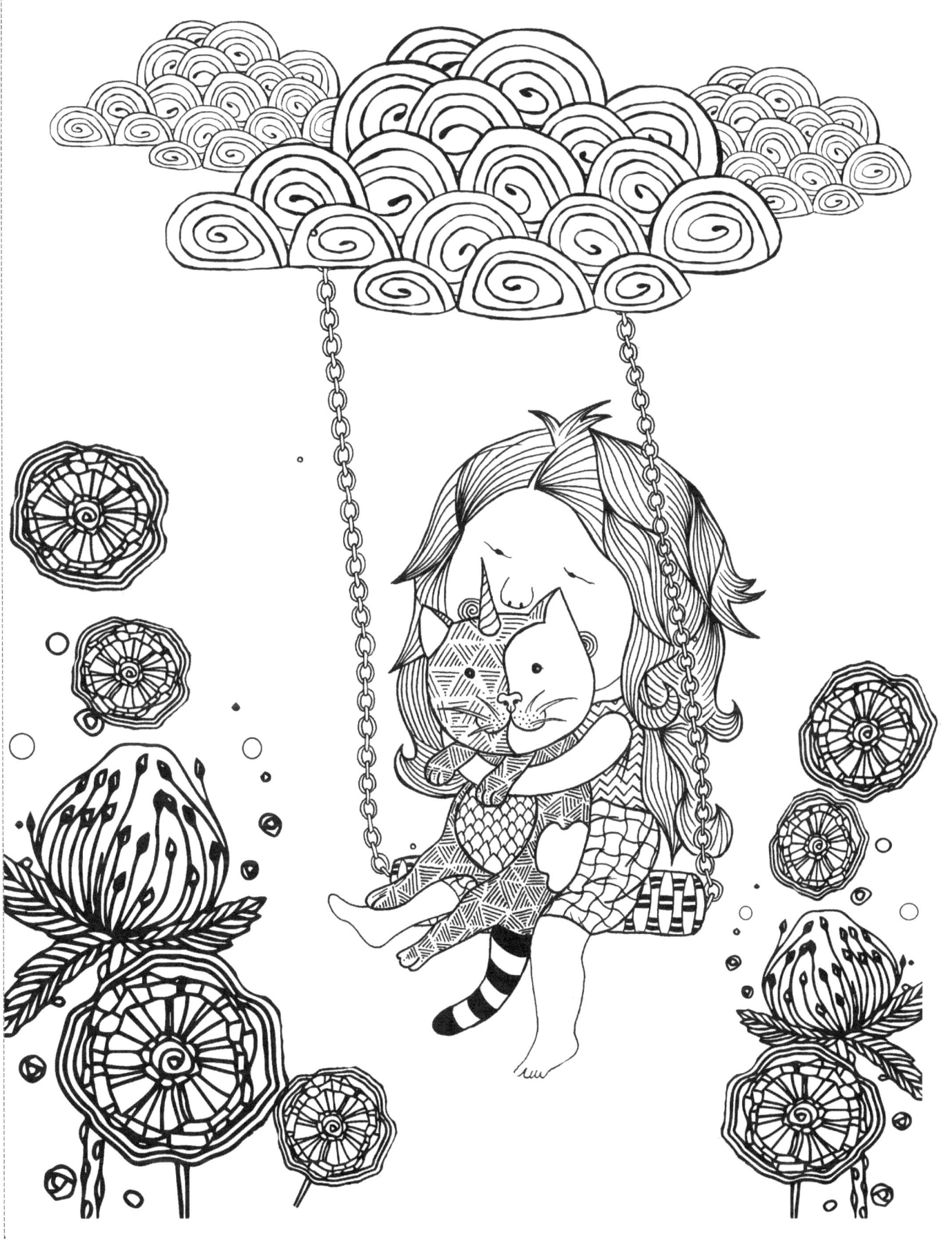

Clouds come floating into my life, no longer to carry rain or usher storm, but to add color to my sunset sky.

Rabindranath Tagore

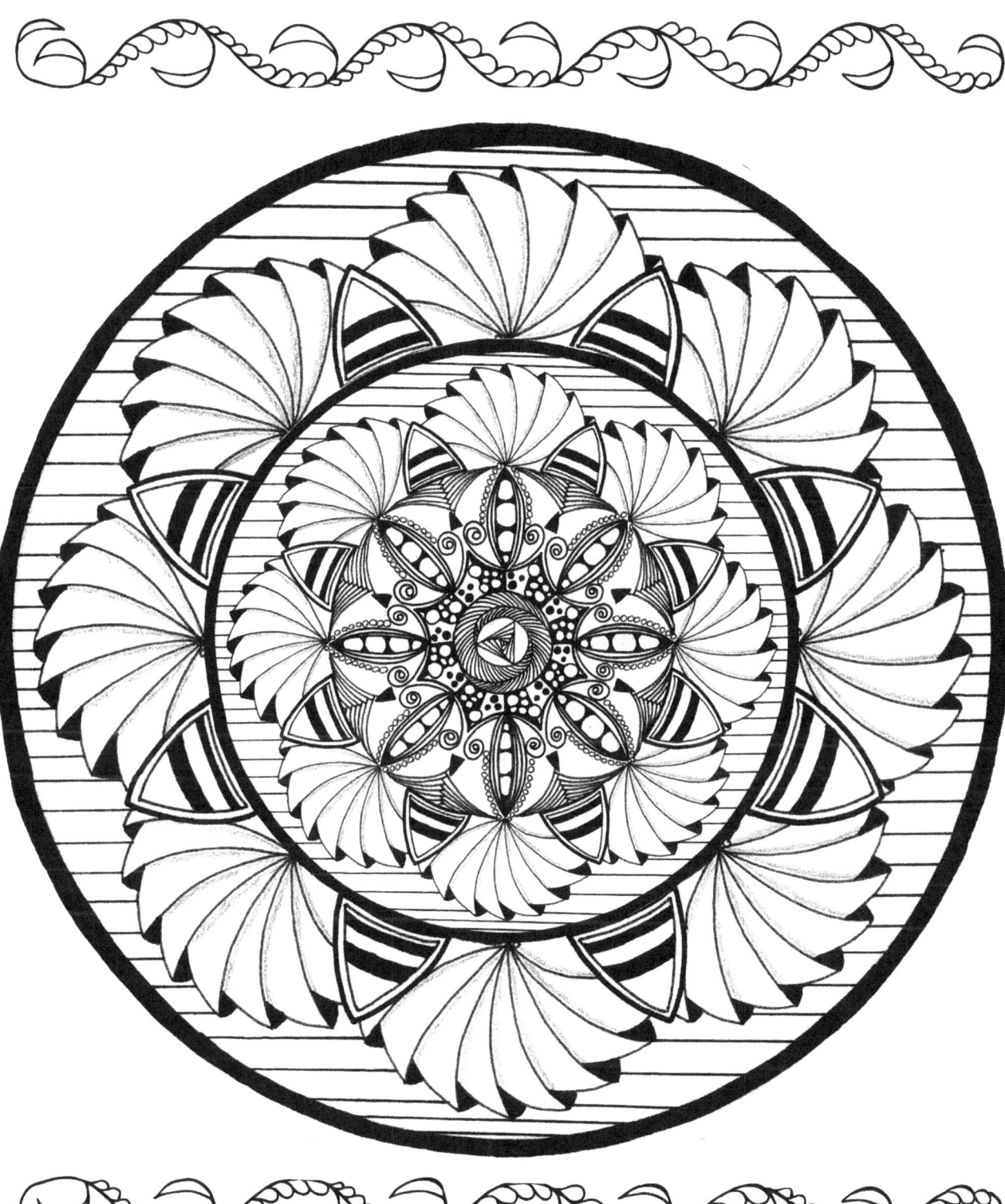

Start by doing what's necessary; then do what's possible;
and suddenly you are doing the impossible.
Francis of Assisi

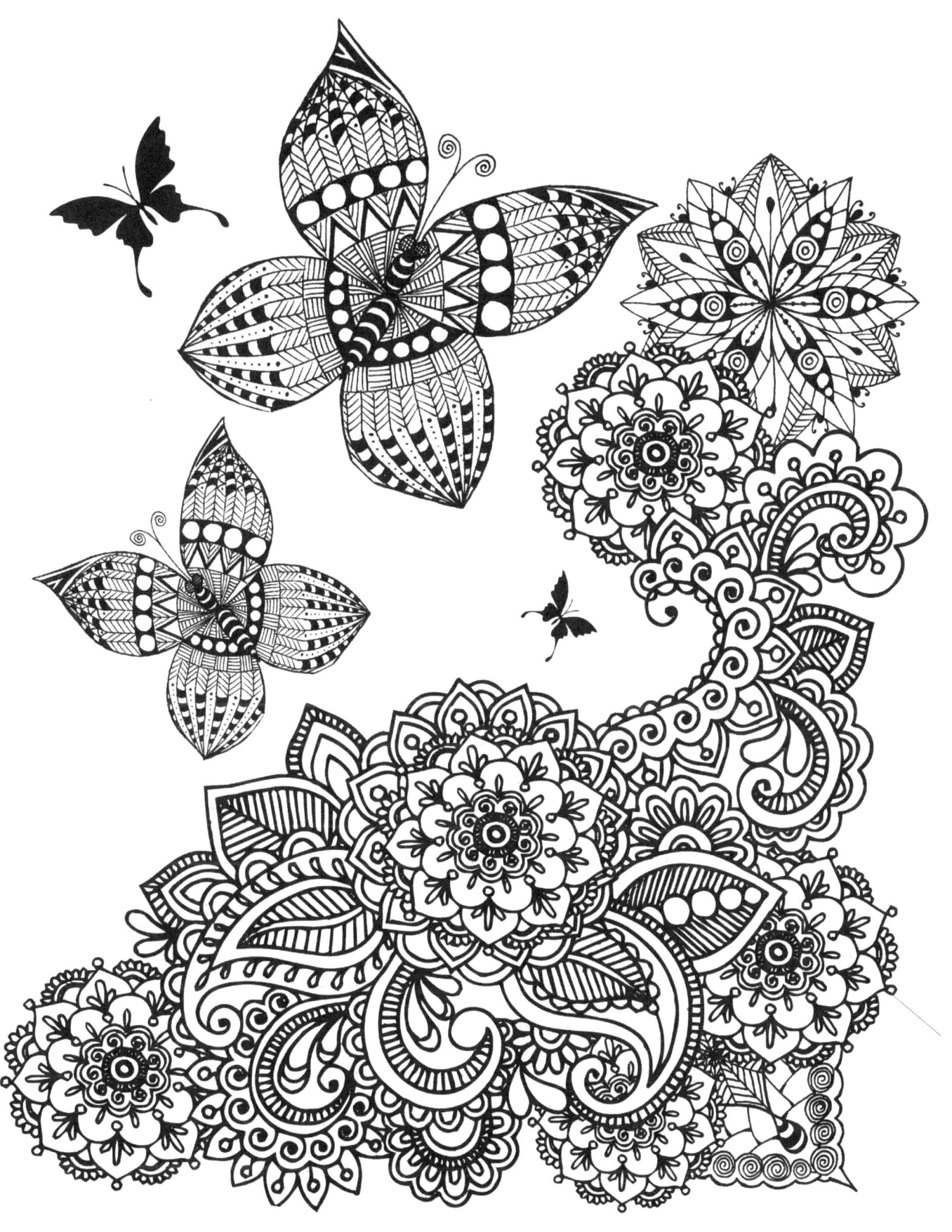

Let your life lightly dance on the edges of Time like
dew on the tip of a leaf.
Rabindranath Tagore

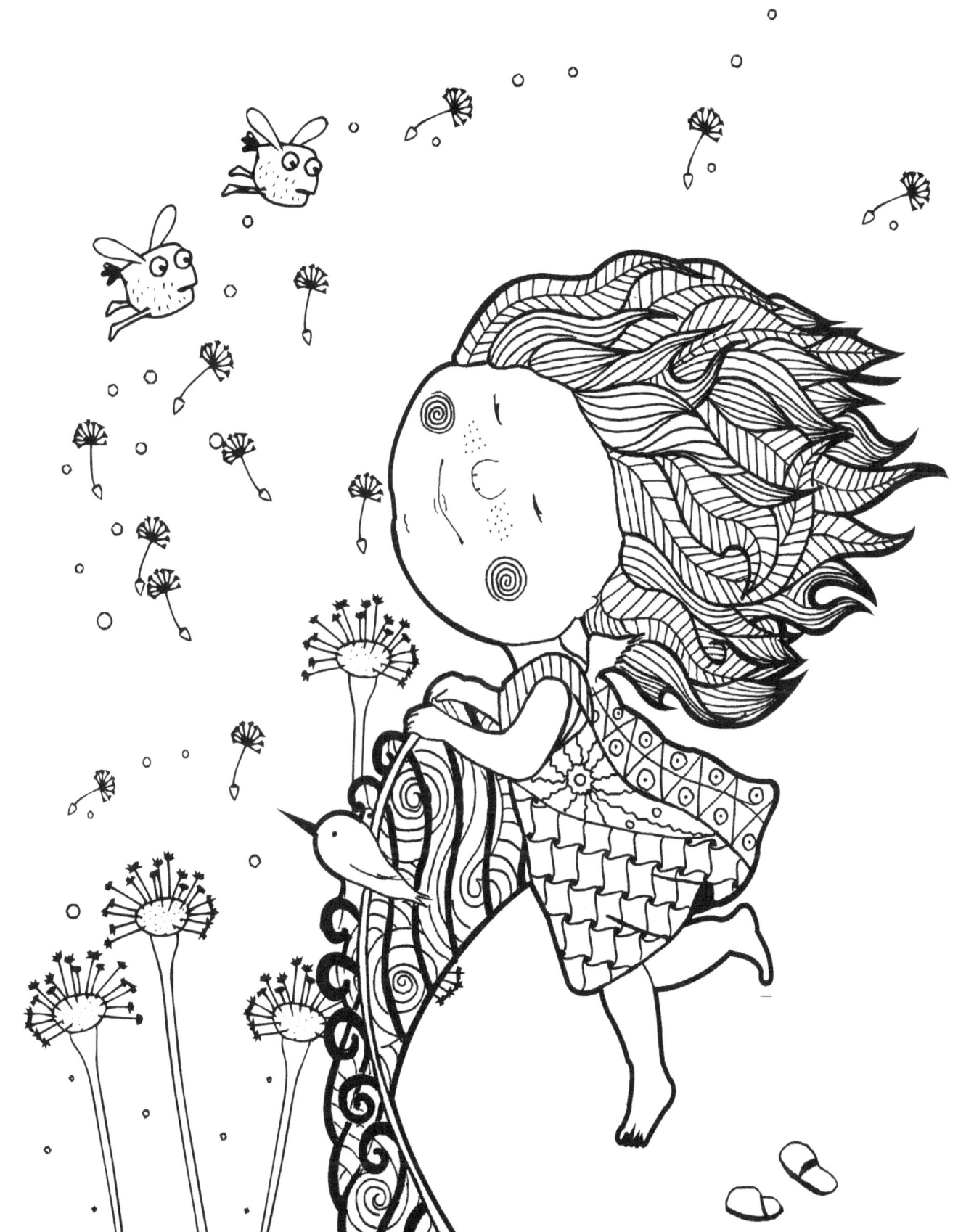

Thousands of candles can be lighted from a single candle,
and the life of the candle will not be shortened.
Happiness never decreases by being shared.
Buddha

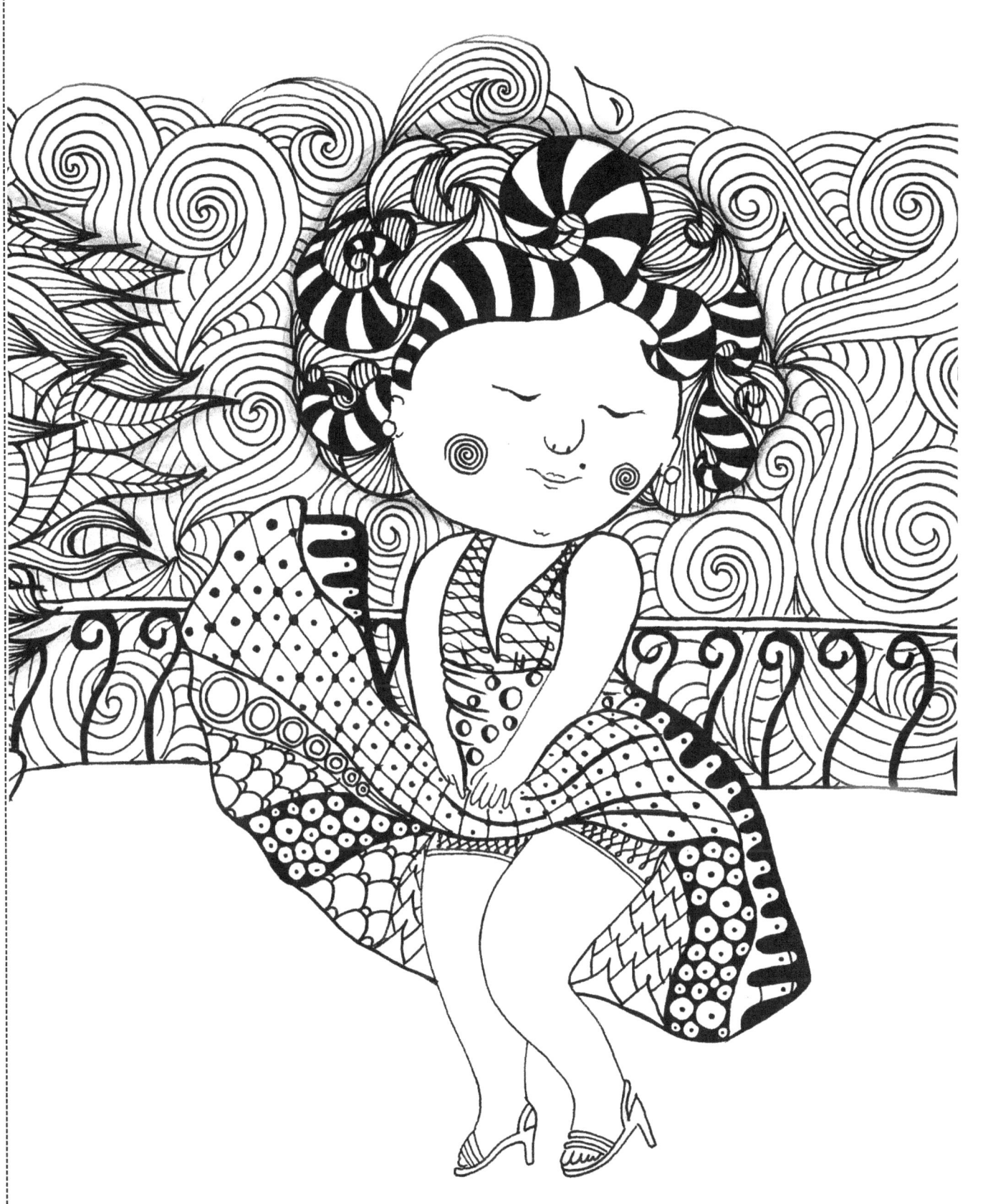

Learn from yesterday, live for today, hope for tomorrow.
The important thing is not to stop questioning.
Albert Einstein

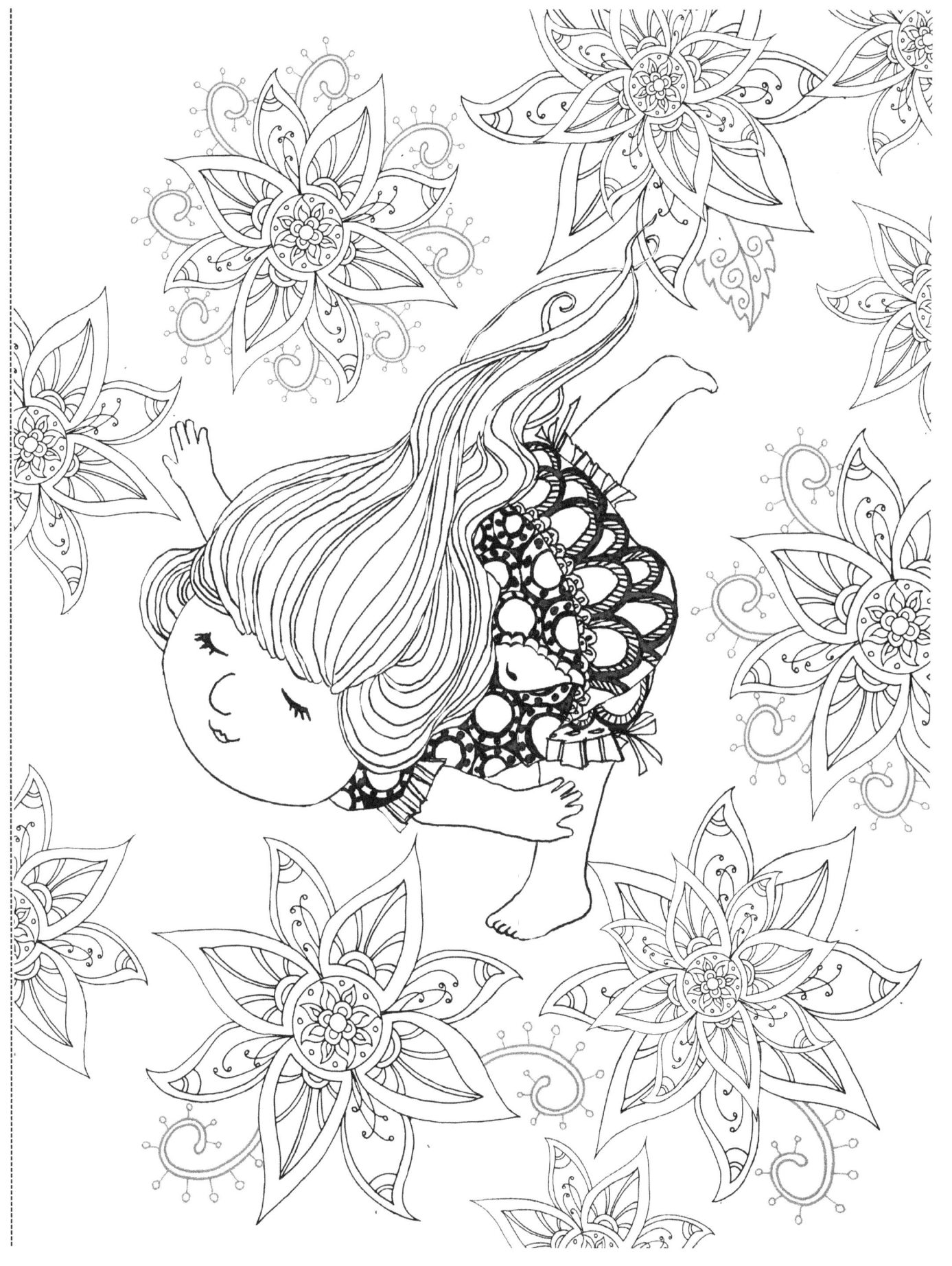

It does not matter how slowly you go as long as you do not stop.
Confucius

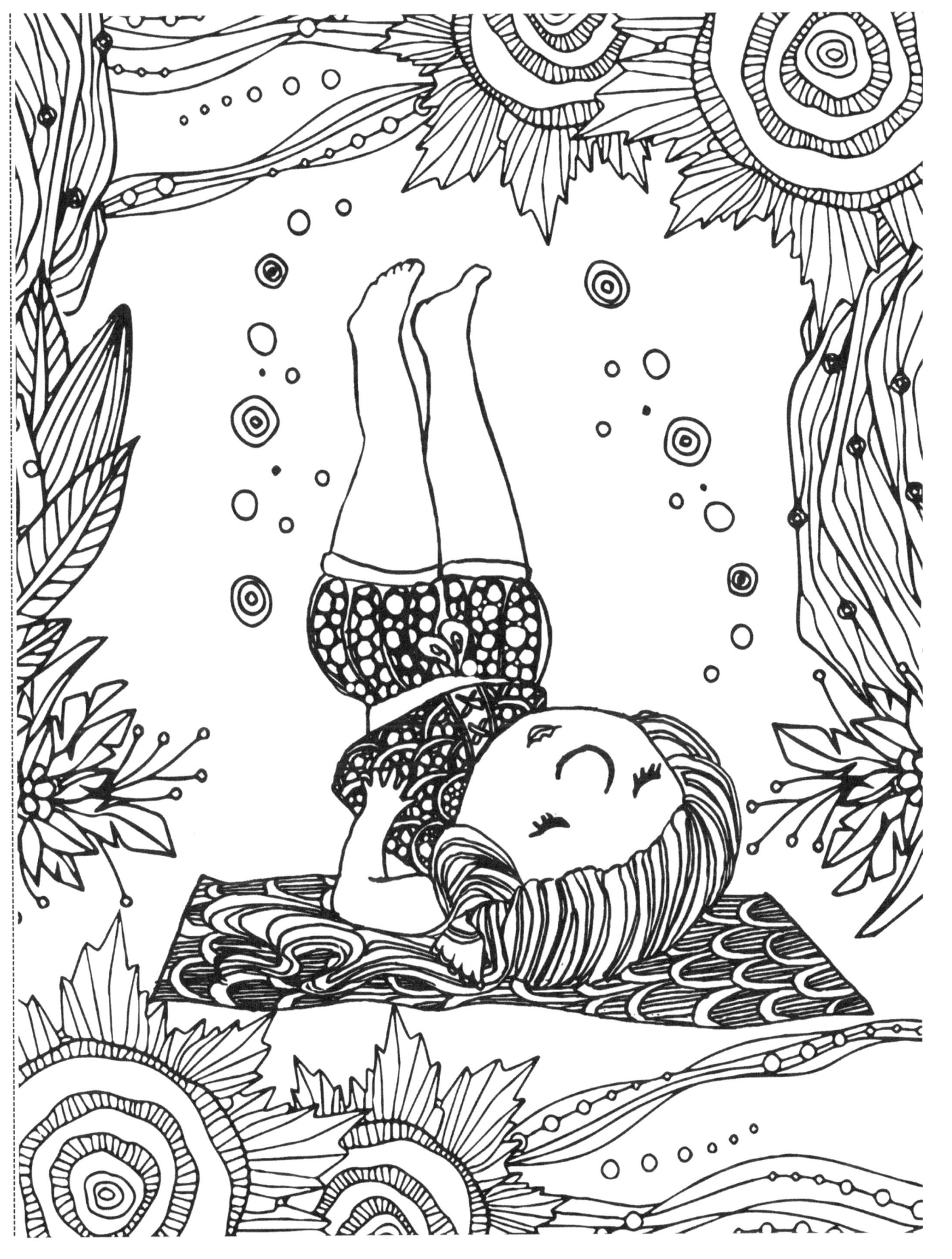

Choose a job you love, and you will never have to work a day in your life.
Confucius

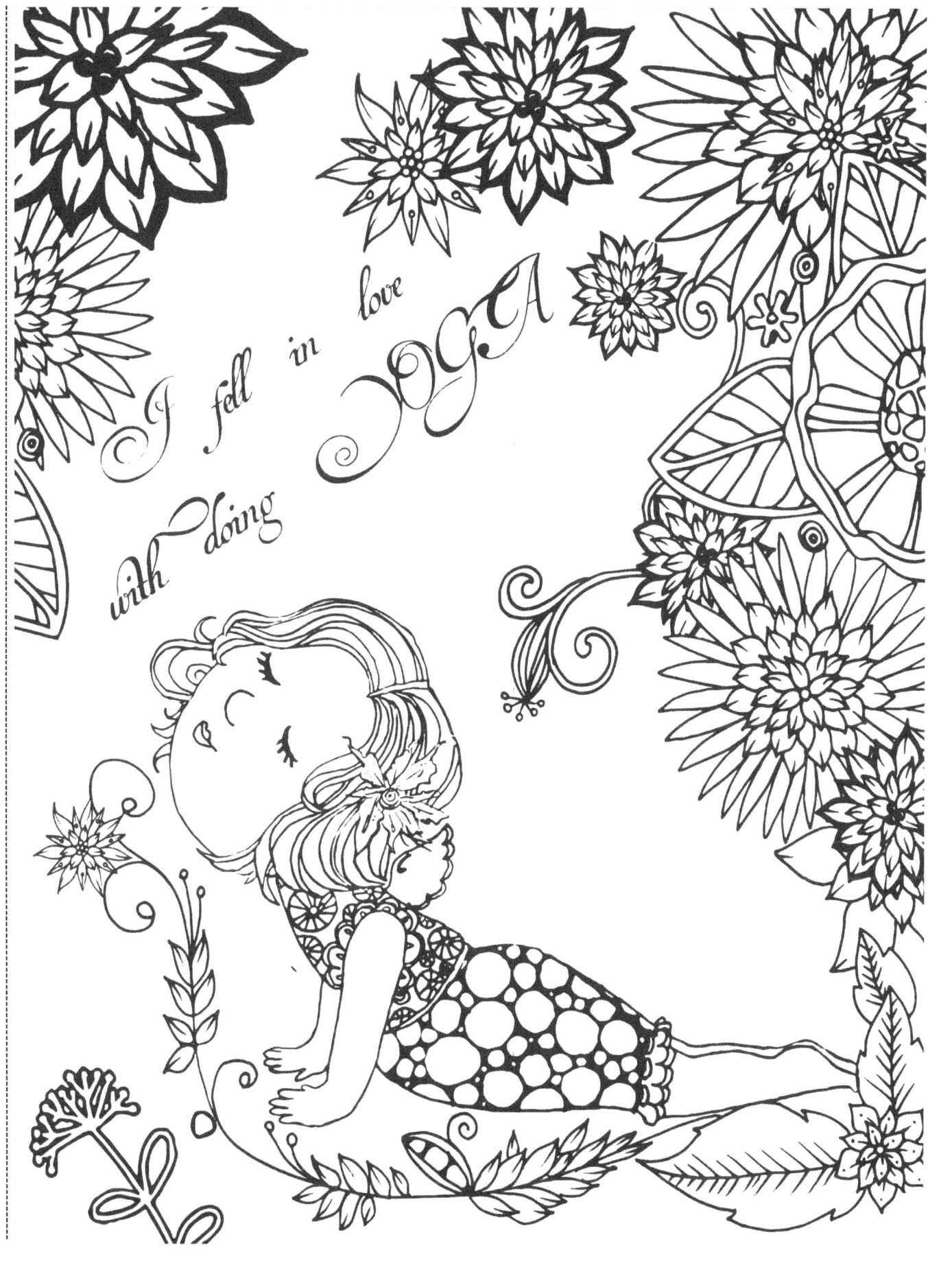

You can't depend on your eyes when your imagination is out of focus.
Mark Twain

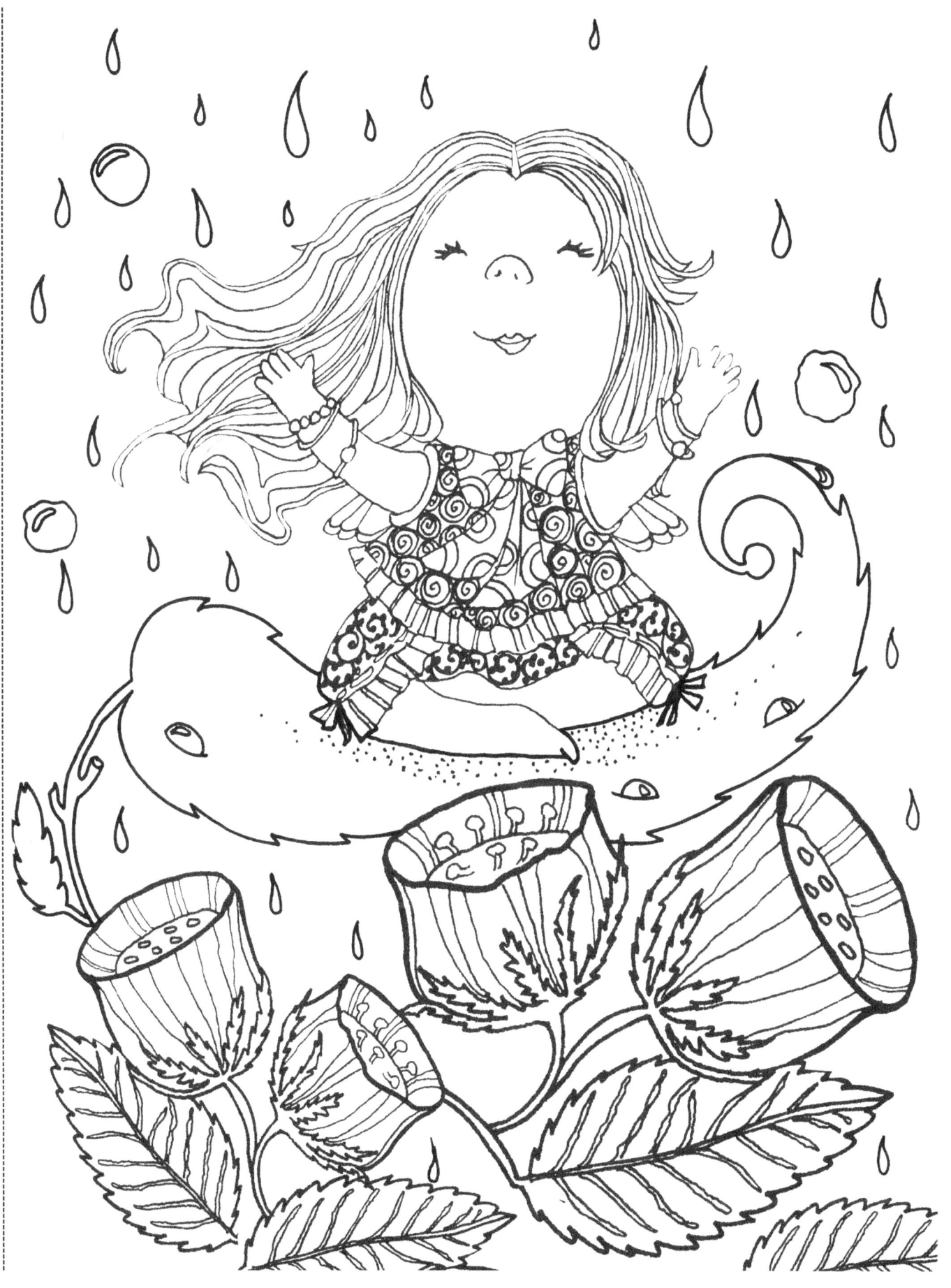

To know what you know and what you do not know,
that is true knowledge.
Confucius

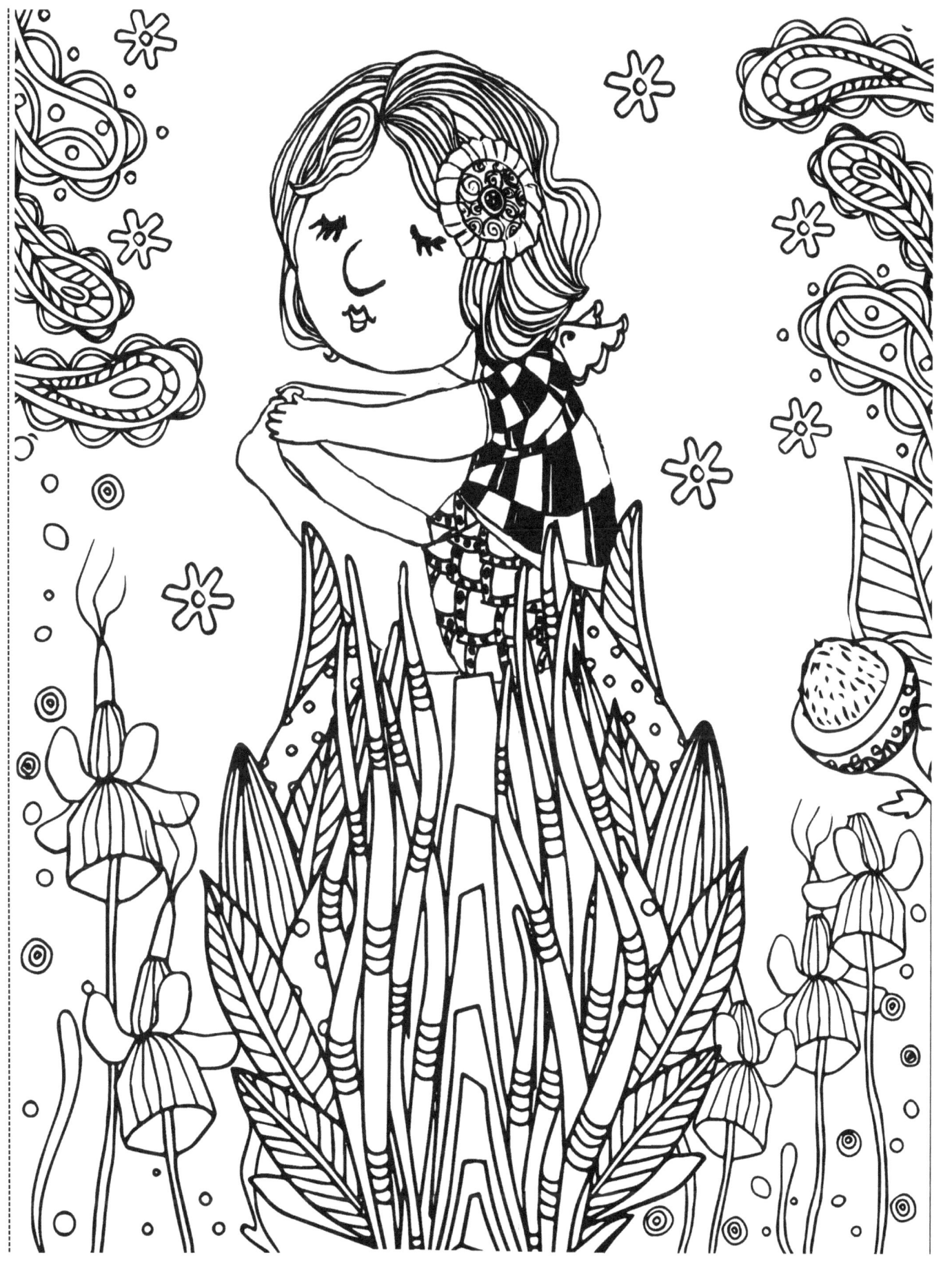

Let us always meet each other with smile,
for the smile is the beginning of love.
Mother Teresa

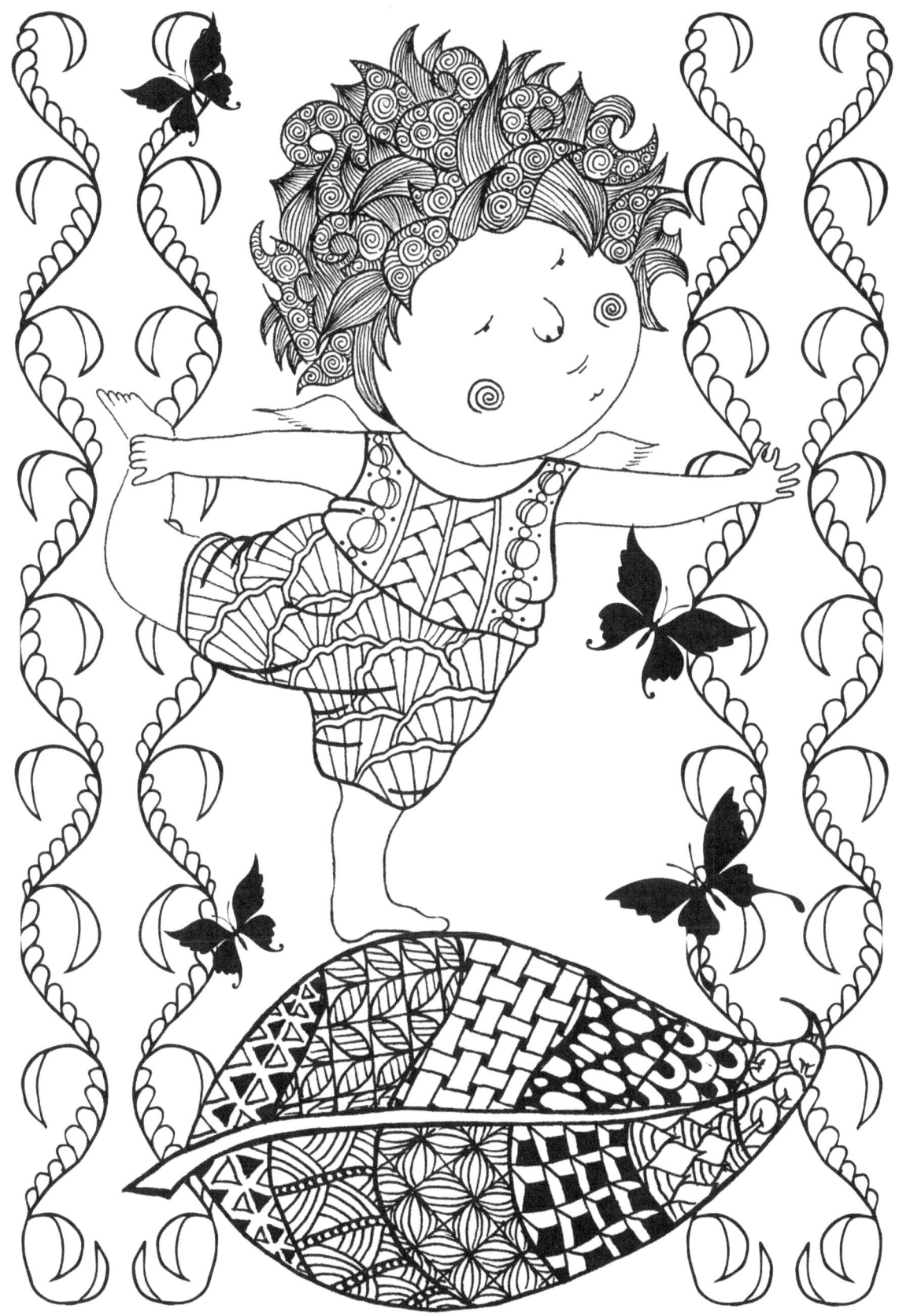

A work of art is above all an adventure of the mind.
Eugene Ionesco

SWEET RAINBOW PROCEDURES:

Tips on Making Complementary Colors Work for You

$\mathcal{N}$owadays coloring books are so popular. But many people can't combine colours very well or perfectly and consequently what this error create is failure in the results this messy rainbow formation in your coloured picture doesn't make it beautiful at the end and you wonder why isn't the result beautiful even after you had spent you important moments working on the colour project. So, either, zendoodle, zentangle, colouring, tangle, patterns or what have you, we have got you covered with our exceptional ideas on improving your zendoodle, zentangle, colouring, tangle, patterns and other colour projects.

COLOUR THEORY

$\mathcal{W}$hen we talking about colours, in the subject of visual arts, color theory is a descriptive body of practical illustration to color mixing and the outcome or visual effects of a specific colour combination.

Also, there are definitions (or categorical segments) of colors based on the contemporary color wheel:
1.The primary colour
2.Secondary colour and
3.Tertiary colour

FACTS ABOUT COLOUR THEORIES

$\mathcal{T}$here are some ancient facts about colour theories which should bring to note. As a matter of fact, the reasons many of us have been messing up some of our art or colour projects is because we have refused to familiarize ourselves with some of these ancient facts and fully infuse the understanding of these facts into our colouring procedures.

The fact we wish to check includes the following;

The establishments of pre-twentieth century shading hypothesis were worked around "unadulterated" or perfect hues, portrayed by tactile encounters instead of properties of the physical world. This has prompted various errors in conventional shading hypothesis rule that are not generally helped in present day formulations. The most essential issue has been a disarray between the conduct of light blends, called added substance.

•   The second issue has been the inability to portray the essential impacts of solid luminance (delicacy) contrasts in the presence of hues reflected from a surface, (for example, paints or inks) instead of shades of light; "hues, for example, tans or ochre's can't show up in blends of light. Subsequently, a solid gentility contrast between a mid-esteemed yellow paint and an encompassing brilliant white makes the yellow give off an impression of being green or cocoa, while a solid splendor contrast between a rainbow and the encompassing sky makes the yellow in a rainbow have all the earmarks of being a fainter yellow, or white.

•   The third issue in the colour theory has been the inclination to portray shading impacts comprehensively or completely, for instance as a differentiation amongst "yellow" and "blue" imagined as nonexclusive hues, when most shading impacts are because of differences on three relative characteristics that characterize all hues.

*I*n summary, our three key factors which are analyzed for constant consideration when handling your paint and colour projects (like zendoodle, zentangle, colouring, coloring, tangle, patterns) includes:

- daintiness (light versus dim, or white versus dark),

- immersion (extraordinary versus dull), and

- tone (e.g., red, orange, yellow, green, blue or purple).

In this manner, the visual effect of "yellow" versus "blue" tints in visual configuration relies on upon the relative daintiness and immersion of the shades.

These perplexities are halfway authentic, and emerged in logical instability about shading recognition that was not determined until the late nineteenth century, when the aesthetic ideas were at that point dug in. Be that as it may, they likewise emerge from the endeavor to depict the exceptionally logical and adaptable conduct of shading recognition regarding unique shading vibes that can be created comparably by any visual media.

Numerous authentic "shading scholars" have expected that three "unadulterated" essential hues can blend all conceivable hues, and that any disappointment of particular paints or inks to match this perfect execution is because of the polluting influence or defect of the colorants. As a general rule, just nonexistent "essential hues" utilized as a part of colorimetric can "blend" or measure all noticeable (perceptually conceivable) hues; yet to do this, these fanciful primaries are characterized as lying outside the scope of obvious hues; i.e., they can't be seen. Any three genuine "essential" shades of light, paint or ink can blend just a constrained scope of hues, called an array, which is constantly littler (contains less hues) than the full scope of hues human can perceive.

COLOUR SUGGESTIONS

*I*n conclusive summary, for your zendoodle, zentangle, colouring, coloring, tangle, patterns and other art projects the following are few colour suggestions we have for you;

It has been discovered and formed into an idea when it comes to colour projects that it is only ideal that colors which lie opposite to one another on the colour wheel, or the set of 'complementary colors', are especially admirable together. Scientific facts have also justified this fact that these colours always look perfect when used together.

BLUE AND PINK

Either baby pink, sky blue, deep blue, deep pink and all other shades, when applied rightly in the normal proportions, these two colours gives you a super result any day.

YELLOW AND PURPLE

When you feel these two colours in a project, zendoodle, zentangle, colouring, tangle, patterns and more, the results is something unique.

YELLOW AND RED

Yellow and green are so hot together; some popular brands have included these two colours in their logos also in the past. When using yellow and red as a complementary colour in a project, the artist can never go wrong.

GREEN AND RED
Green and red brings something bogus to mind but the truth is, these two colours might seem bold but when used in the right proportions for any art project, the results remains heart melting

RED AND WHITE
Red and white, sounds like love… it's not just Valentine's Day themed colour. These colour combination could be merged into your Mandalay projects or any art projects including zendoodle, zentangle, colouring, tangle, patterns and more.
Blue and red
This is the colour of the American flag. Now you can't deny that the US flag hasn't been well designed.

*T*here are many more colours we could suggest but you need to use this ideas we have for you in this article then remain creative to discover more innovative colour combinations' you can include in your art and colour based projects, maybe you can tell us what you discovered too!

*E*njoy sweet rainbow procedures in your art works…

Sincerely yours,
Lana Karr and Olga Dee

For more beautiful articles with this type of amazing content on zendoodle, zentangle, colouring, tangle, patterns please follow the links:

WEB: http://doodleartclub.com/
FACEBOOK: https://www.facebook.com/doodleartclub/
INSTAGRAM: https://www.instagram.com/doodleartclub/

ABOUT THE AUTHORS

ABOUT THE AUTHORS

$\mathcal{L}$ana Karr is interested in meditation and ways to help people to de-stress. Having participated in numerous retreats, she has a strong passion to help people combat stress from their busy lives. She has always been looking for creative ways to help people de-stress and forget their sorrows through meditation. On her journey to help people, she realized the experience of doodle art was very similar to meditation. She noticed that while people claimed they couldn't draw, they doodled artistic pieces, naturally, without even giving effort. And that's when she realized the potential of doodle art to reach meditative state of mind.

$\mathcal{O}$lga Dee, a Russian art school graduate and an art teacher, noticed positive health benefits of drawing during her art-teaching career. She has been working closely with people of all age groups, since 2005, and found out how drawing had positive effects on her students' lives. Having interest in Ayurveda medicine for years, she always had a determination to combine meditation with drawing to encourage her students to draw from their souls, instead of just copying from others' artwork.

FIND US :

Facebook www.facebook.com/doodleartclub
Instagram www.instagram.com/doodleartclub
Web www.doodleartclub.com
YouTube www.youtube.com/c/doodleartclub

www.ingramcontent.com/pod-product-compliance
Lightning Source LLC
Chambersburg PA
CBHW081746170526
45167CB00009B/3943